THE BRAMBLY HEDGE
PATTERN BOOK

JILL BARKLEM'S
characters created in fabric by
SUE DOLMAN

COLLINS

If you look very hard amongst the tangled roots and stems of Brambly Hedge, you may see the small front doors and windows of the mice who live there. Old Oak Palace is the home of Lord and Lady Woodmouse and their small daughter, Primrose. Mr and Mrs Apple live at Crabapple Cottage and Wilfred Toadflax lives next door in the hornbeam tree. Dusty Dogwood's flour mill is down by the stream and Poppy Eyebright can be found at the Dairy Stump.

It is a busy, self-sufficient little community and although the mice work hard throughout the year gathering food, cooking and preserving, improving their homes and using all the natural resources to the full, they still have plenty of time for fun. There are summer weddings to celebrate, like the time Dusty Dogwood and Poppy Eyebright exchanged their vows aboard a floating raft, birthday picnics for the children, Snow Balls when conditions are right, and wild strawberry and autumn berry picking expeditions.

Children love the Brambly Hedge stories and these easy-to-follow instructions and patterns enable you to make charming fabric versions of the mice for them to enjoy.

THE BRAMBLY HEDGE BOOKS

by Jill Barklem

Spring Story · Summer Story · Autumn Story · Winter Story

The Secret Staircase · The High Hills

The Four Seasons of Brambly Hedge

Photographs on pages 4 and 5, 11, 13, 21, 23, 29, 31, 41, 43, 49, 51 and front and back cover by Ian Wood

First published 1984

Fourth impression 1988

© Brambly Hedge Jill Barklem 1980
© Volume Copyright William Collins Sons & Co Ltd 1984
© Text and diagrams Sue Dolman 1984

ISBN 0 00 183977 2

Origination by Culver Graphic Ltd
Printed in Hong Kong by Imago

Contents

General instructions

For the best results, cutting and stitching must be accurate.

PATTERNS All patterns are printed full size. Using tracing paper, carefully trace over each one marking position of eyes, waist lines and other details. Cut out tracings.

CUTTING FABRIC Read instructions on pattern pieces. Some felt and all fur patterns have no seam allowances. Place your tracings of these patterns onto fabric and draw round them with a fine felt pen. Stitch on the line before cutting out.
Mark eye positions and other details by making a pin hole in the tracing pattern and marking through. Arrows indicate the directions of stripes or fur pile. Pin patterns to appropriate fabric. Always note whether a piece is to be cut once or twice or turned over to make a pair. Scissors must be sharp.

JOINING FABRIC Match pieces with right sides together. Fold hems onto wrong side.

SEAMS, HEMS AND GATHERS All these are 6 mm ($\frac{1}{4}$ in) from the edge, unless otherwise stated. The edges of some seams will need to be trimmed close to the stitching to reduce the bulk of the seam.

STITCHING You can stitch by machine or by hand using a tiny neat running stitch. Stitching the head to the body and skirt to the body will be easier if you use a long fine darning needle.

FILLING Use a white synthetic toy filling. Fill with small pinches at a time gradually building up the shape. Use hands to mould into shape from the outside whilst filling.

GLUE Flowers, leaves and bows will need to be glued into position. Use a clear adhesive (Bostik 1). Apply small amounts of glue with the point of a pin.

BUYING FABRICS To help when buying fabrics, the measurements given allow for the patterns to be placed in a row across the width of the fabric. The first measurement is the width, the second is the depth. This does not apply to felt which is usually sold by the square.

SAFETY The mice are not suitable for babies or very young children because of the beads and small decorative accessories.

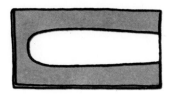 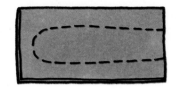 

1 HANDS
Position pattern onto
double felt. Draw around.

2 Stitch on the line leaving
end open.

3 Cut out close to stitching.

HOW TO TURN HANDS, TAILS AND FEET

From a D.I.Y. or woodworking shop, purchase two pieces of hardwood
dowel approximately 25 cm (10 in) long and 3 mm ($\frac{1}{8}$ in) diameter.
File the ends flat and smooth.

 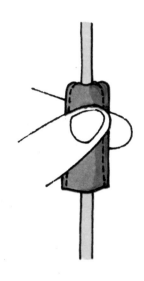 

4 Slide the first dowel into
the hand. Press the second
dowel onto the top of the
hand against the top of the
first dowel.

5 With moistened fingers,
gently roll the hand
upwards over the second
dowel. Roll until turned
inside out.

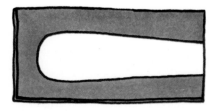 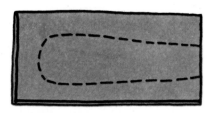

6 FEET
Position pattern onto
double felt. Draw around.

7 Stitch on the line leaving ·
end open. Cut out.

8 Turn onto right side using dowel. Bend a pipe cleaner double. Push bend inside foot.

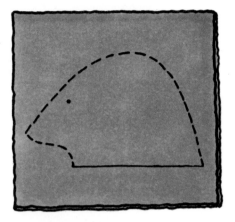

9 HEAD
Cut two 115 mm (4½ in) squares of fur fabric. Brush pile in its natural direction. Match squares with right sides together and pile on both running from left to right. Lay head pattern centrally with nose on the left side. Draw around. Mark eye.

10 Stitch on the line leaving the neck open. Position pattern onto the other side of fur. If the stitched shape on the other side is a fraction bigger than the pattern, match the pattern to the stitched line between the nose and the top of the head. Mark eye.

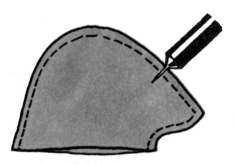

11 Cut around head and across bottom line. Mark eyes again with a fine felt pen gently pushing the tip through the fabric until a mark can be seen on the right side. Turn head onto right side.

12 Fill head comfortably up to the opening, rounding out the back and the cheeks. Gather around the opening with strong thread. Pull tightly to close. Scratch the back seam with a needle to release caught pile.

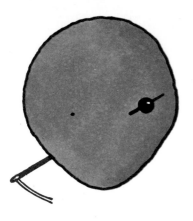 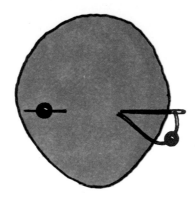 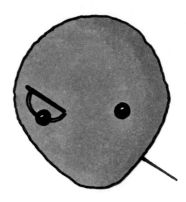

13 EYES
With a long needle and strong thread, take a stitch from the gathered area of the head to the eye mark. Attach bead.

14 Take needle across to other eye mark. Attach bead.

15 Take needle back to gathered area to fasten off. Stroke fur pile behind beads with the point of a needle.

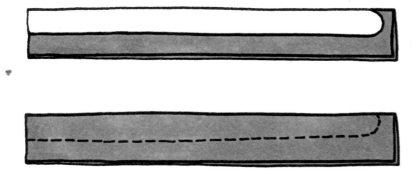

16 TAIL
Position tail pattern against the fold on double felt. Draw around.

17 Stitch on the line, leaving the end open. Cut out. Turn onto right side using the dowel.

Instructions for Mrs Apple, Primrose and Poppy Eyebright.

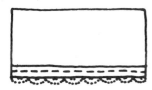 

18 TAIL FRILL
Fold one long edge onto wrong side. Iron. Position guipure lace onto right side overlapping the fold. Stitch.

19 Fold to match sides. Stitch. Trim away edge. Turn onto right side.

20 Thread frill onto open end of tail.

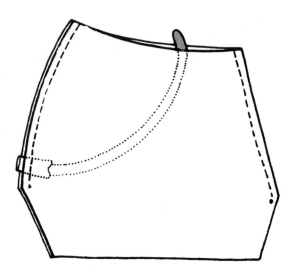

21 PANTALOONS
Match pieces with tail between and frilled end positioned in the back seam as marked on pattern. Stitch down to spots.

22 Fold to match inside legs. Stitch. Turn onto right side.

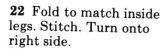

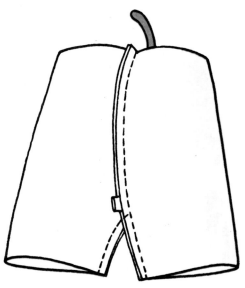

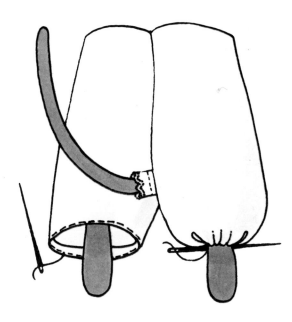

23 Gather around leg. Fold edge inside on gathers. Position foot into leg with 32 mm (1¼ in) showing. Pull up gathers tight. Stitch through the foot at gathers. Bend feet forward.

Primrose Woodmouse

Primrose Woodmouse is the daughter of Lord and Lady
Woodmouse. She lives in the Old Oak Palace. She is
a lively small mouse and loves to explore with her good
friend, Wilfred Toadflax.

Patterns

All patterns are printed full size. Using tracing paper, carefully trace over each one marking positions of eyes and other details. Cut out tracings.

Foot

Stitch before cutting out

Beige felt

Cut foot from doubled fabric.

Pantaloons

Cut out a pair

White cotton

Tail position

Apron

Cut out 1

White cotton

Pocket position

Materials

1 Two pipe cleaners.
2 White cotton fabric 64 cm × 15 cm (25 in × 6 in).
3 Brown fur fabric 23 cm × 11.4 cm (9 in × 4½ in).
   Dense pile no more than 8 mm (5⁄16 in) deep.
4 Primrose-coloured cotton 84 cm × 15 cm (33 in × 6 in).
   This allows for both skirt pieces to be cut from double fabric.
5 White satin ribbon 31 cm (12 in) long, 6 mm (¼ in) wide.
6 Broderie anglaise lace 1 m (39 in) long, 22 mm (7⁄8 in) wide.
7 Two black beads (very tiny).
8 Two black beads 6 mm (¼ in) diameter.
9 Beige felt 23 cm × 23 cm (9 in × 9 in).
10 Guipure lace 50 mm (2 in) long, 10 mm (3⁄8 in) wide.
    Glue and toy filling.

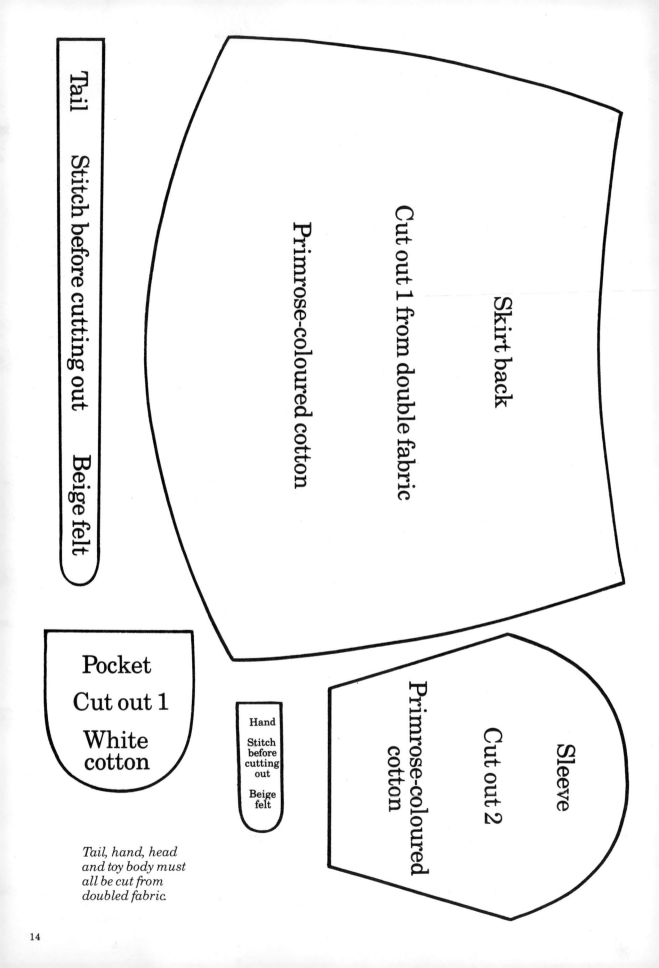

Tail   Stitch before cutting out   Beige felt

Skirt back

Cut out 1 from double fabric

Primrose-coloured cotton

Pocket

Cut out 1

White cotton

Hand

Stitch before cutting out

Beige felt

Sleeve

Cut out 2

Primrose-coloured cotton

Tail, hand, head and toy body must all be cut from doubled fabric.

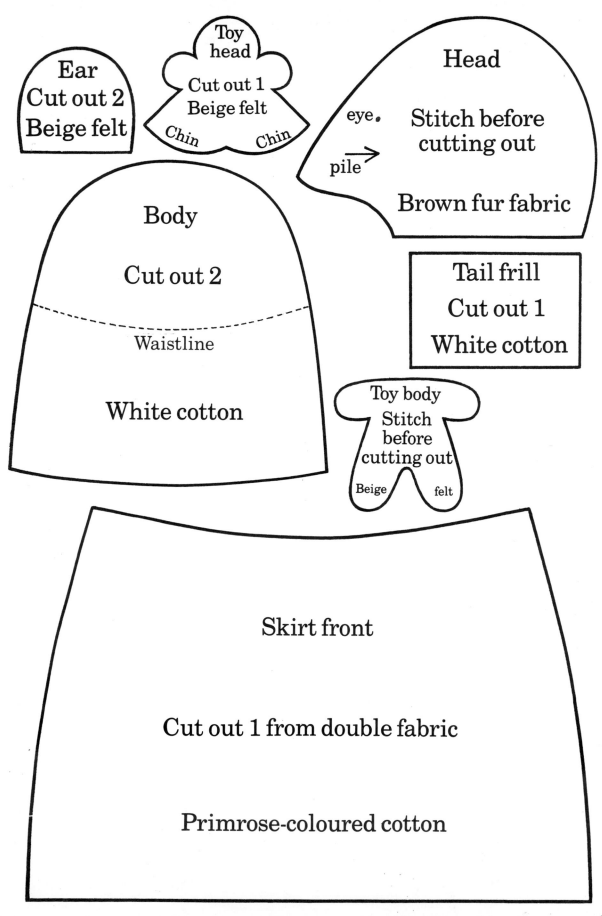

Ear
Cut out 2
Beige felt

Toy
head
Cut out 1
Beige felt
Chin   Chin

Head

eye.
pile →
Stitch before
cutting out

Brown fur fabric

Body

Cut out 2

Waistline

White cotton

Tail frill
Cut out 1
White cotton

Toy body
Stitch
before
cutting out
Beige   felt

Skirt front

Cut out 1 from double fabric

Primrose-coloured cotton

Instructions
for making up

Instructions for head, tail, tail frill, hands, feet and pantaloons on pages 7, 8, 9 and 10. Seams, hems and gathers are 6 mm ($\frac{1}{4}$ in) from the edge. Match pieces with right sides together. Finished height 171 mm ($6\frac{3}{4}$ in).

1 BODY
Match pieces. Stitch. Trim away edge. Turn onto right side.

2 Fill firmly up to edge. Gather around. Pull up tight to close.

3 EARS
Fold ear bottom in half. Stitch on edge.

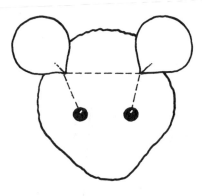

4 Take head and position ears facing forward 25 mm (1 in) above eyes and 38 mm ($1\frac{1}{2}$ in) apart. Pin. Stitch through bottom edge into head. Sit gathered area of head onto body. Beginning with large loose stitches in the centre of both, pull head to body comfortably. Stitch around again.

5 PANTALOONS
Fill legs around pipe cleaners and up to 25 mm (1 in) from the top. Use enough filling to hold shape well. Gather around pantaloon top leaving 38 mm ($1\frac{1}{2}$ in) of the front ungathered. Fold top inside on the gather line. Sit body centrally into pantaloons. Match front pantaloon top to waistline on body. Pin. Add more filling under body if necessary. Push more filling into sides and back.

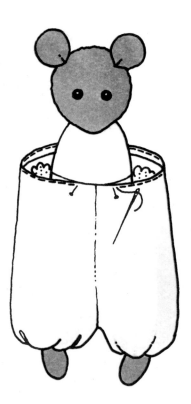

6 Pull up gathers to fit body, matching pantaloon top to waistline. Stitch top to body.

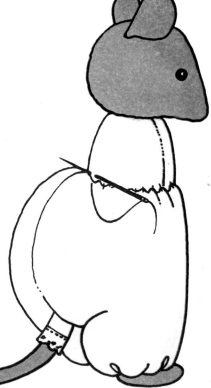

7 SLEEVES
Fold up bottom edge. Iron.

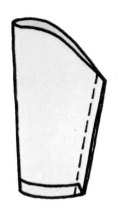

8 Fold to match sides. Stitch. Turn onto right side.

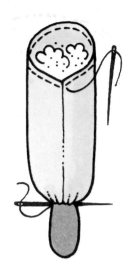

9 Gather around sleeve bottom on the fold. Pop hand inside with 19 mm ($\frac{3}{4}$ in) showing. Pull up tight. Take stitches through hand. Fill sleeve softly. Do not overfill. Gather around top. Pull up tucking edges inside.

10 Bend arm. Stitch.

11 Position arm onto body side. Pin. Stitch through top into body.

12 APRON FRILLS
Cut two pieces of broderie anglaise 152 mm (6 in) long. Fold raw edge of one piece onto wrong side. Iron. Gather across on the fold. Pull up to measure 82 mm ($3\frac{1}{4}$ in). Repeat with other piece of lace.

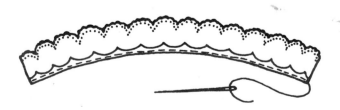

13 Lay gathered lace over shoulders with ends overlapping top of pantaloons. Stitch ends front and back.

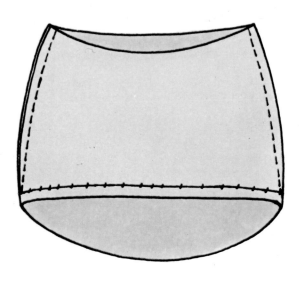

14 SKIRT

To make a better skirt shape, cut pieces from double fabric. Proceed as if using single fabric. Match pieces. Stitch sides. Fold up bottom edge. Stitch. Turn onto right side.

15 Position broderie anglaise lace around skirt bottom, on the wrong side, with curved edge of lace just showing on the right side. Fold short ends of lace over and butt the folds. Stitch. Gather around top of skirt, leaving 38 mm (1½ in) of the front ungathered.

16 Pin hands out of the way. Slip skirt onto Primrose. Fold skirt top inside on gathers. Pin front to body. Pull up gathers to fit body tightly over pantaloons. Stitch skirt top to body.

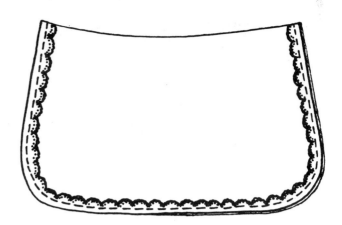

17 BOW
Cut a piece of
ribbon 31 cm
(12 in) long. Tie
bow. Glue bow to
waist at centre
back.

18 APRON
Cut a piece of broderie anglaise lace
36 cm (14 in) long. Trim lace to measure
only 13 mm ($\frac{1}{2}$ in) at widest point. Match
raw edge of lace to apron edge on the
right side. Ease around curves with tiny
tucks. Stitch. Trim away edge. Iron lace
flat.

◁ **19 POCKET**
Fold over top edge. Iron. Gather around
curve on very edge. Pull up gathers
enough to turn edge onto wrong side.

20 Position pocket onto apron. Stitch.
Gather across apron top. Fold over on
gathers. Pull up to measure 82 mm ($3\frac{1}{4}$ in).

◁ **21** Place apron on Primrose. Pin. Stitch
apron top to body.

22 TOY Body
Position body pattern onto double felt. Draw around.

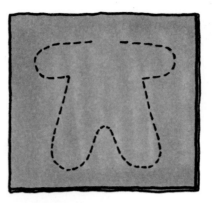

23 Stitch on the line, leaving the top open.

24 Cut out close to stitchin Turn onto right side.

25 TOY Head
Fold in half to match chin. Stitch on the edge. Do not turn inside out.

26 Fill head.

27 Fold back of head dowr to close over filling, leaving ears standing out. Stitch or edge.

28 Stitch tiny beads to face. Make a nose with a few stitches of dark thread.

29 Fill body with extra filling in the tummy. Gather around opening. Pull up tight.

30 Stitch head to body. Stitch arms to sides. Decide how Primrose will hold the toy. Stitch the back of the toy to Primrose and Primrose's hand to the front of the toy. Tidy her fur with a brush.

Wilfred Toadflax

*Wilfred and his brother and sisters live in the hornbeam tree.
Wilfred has a habit of getting into scrapes and his father
often has to confiscate his catapult.*

Patterns

All patterns are printed full size. Using tracing paper, carefully trace over each one, marking positions of eyes and other details. Cut out tracings.

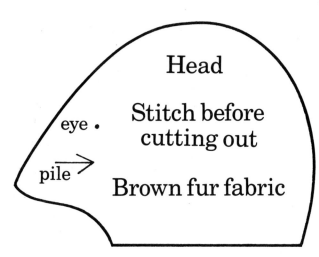

Head

Stitch before cutting out

eye •

pile →

Brown fur fabric

Sleeve

Cut out 2

Striped interlock

Body

Cut out 2

Striped interlock

→

Tail   Stitch before cutting out   Beige felt

**Ear
Cut out 2
Beige felt**

Foot   Stitch before cutting out   Beige felt

Hand   Stitch before cutting out   Beige felt

*Head, tail, hand
and foot must all
be cut from
doubled fabric.*

Materials

1 Striped interlock (tee-shirt fabric) 27 cm × 10 cm (10½ in × 4 in).
The body and arms must be made from a stretchy fabric.
A plain bright red or a sock could be used instead.
2 Brown fur fabric 23 cm × 11.4 cm (9 in × 4½ in).
Dense pile no more than 8 mm (5⁄16 in) deep.
3 Two black beads 6 mm (¼ in) diameter.
4 Two pipe cleaners.
5 Denim (lightweight) 46 cm × 15 cm (18 in × 6 in).
6 Beige felt 18 cm × 18 cm (7 in × 7 in).
7 A forked twig 45 mm (1¾ in). Strong thread and black felt.
Toy filling.

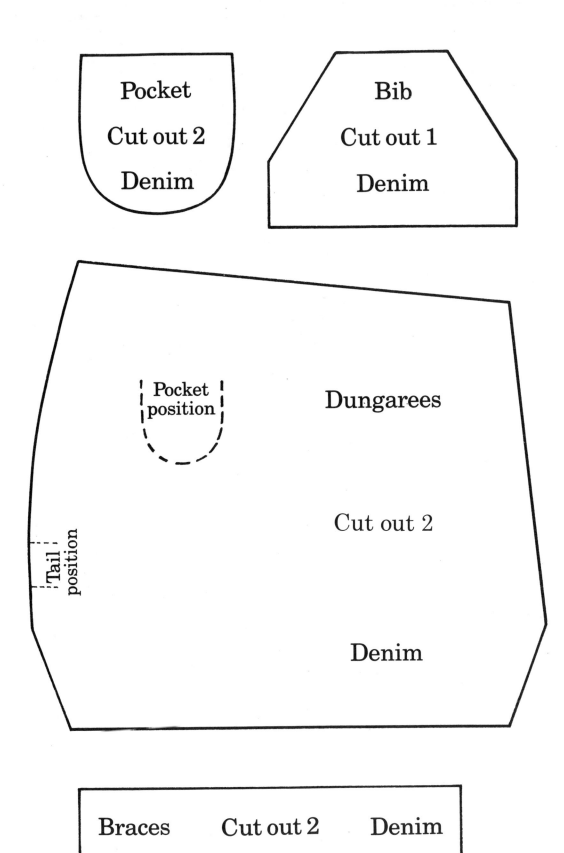

Pocket

Cut out 2

Denim

Bib

Cut out 1

Denim

Pocket
position

Dungarees

Cut out 2

Denim

Tail
position

Braces   Cut out 2   Denim

Instructions
for making up

Instructions for head, tail, hands and feet on pages 7, 8 and 9. Seams, hems and gathers are 6 mm ($\frac{1}{4}$ in) from the edge. Match pieces with right sides together. Finished height 171 mm ($6\frac{3}{4}$ in).

1 BODY
Match pieces. Stitch. Turn onto right side.

2 Fill up to edge. Gather around. Pull up tight to close. The finished body should be the size and shape of a large egg. Mould shape with hands.

3 EARS
Fold ear bottom in half. Stitch on edge.

4 Take head and position ears facing forward 25 mm (1 in) above eyes and 38 mm ($1\frac{1}{2}$ in) apart. Pin. Stitch through bottom edges into head.

5 Sit gathered area of head onto body. Beginning with large loose stitches in the centre of both, pull head to body comfortably. Stitch around again.

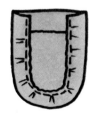

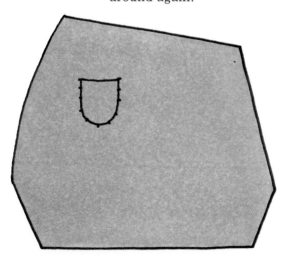

6 POCKETS
Fold over top edge. Iron. Gather around on very edge.

7 Pull up gathers enough to turn edge onto wrong side.

8 DUNGAREES
Position pockets onto dungarees as marked on pattern. Stitch pocket edges. ▷

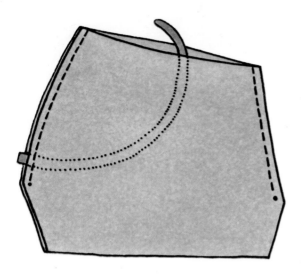

9 Match pieces with tail between and open end of tail positioned in the back seam. Stitch down to spots.

10 Fold to match inside legs. Stitch. Turn onto right side.

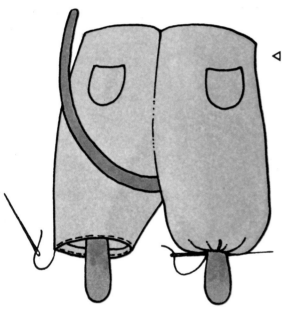

◁ **11** Gather around leg. Fold edge inside on gathers. Position foot into leg with 32 mm (1¼ in) showing. Pull up gathers tight. Stitch through the foot at gathers. Bend feet forward.

12 BRACES
Fold one piece into three lengthways, hiding raw edge at the back. Stitch through centre. Repeat with other piece.

13 Lay braces over shoulders, crossing at the back. Stitch ends to body.

14 Fill legs around pipe ▷ cleaners and up to 25 mm (1 in) from the top. Use enough filling to hold shape well. Gather around dungaree top leaving 38 mm (1½ in) of the front ungathered. Fold top inside on the gather line. Sit body centrally into dungarees with 35 mm (1⅜ in) showing. Pin. Add more filling under body if necessary. Push more filling into sides and back.

◁ **15** Pull up gathers to fit body. Stitch dungaree top to body.

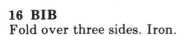

16 BIB
Fold over three sides. Iron.

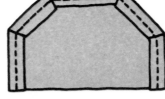

17 Fold over two corners. Iron. Stitch around with white thread, showing stitching on the right side.

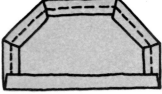

18 Fold up bottom edge. Iron.

19 Position bib onto Wilfred. Pin. Stitch across bottom on fold and through top corners.

20 SLEEVES
Fold up bottom edge.

21 Fold to match sides. Stitch. Turn onto right side.

22 Gather around sleeve ▷ bottom on the fold. Pop hand inside with 20 mm ($\frac{3}{4}$ in) showing. Pull up tight. Take stitches through the hand. Fill sleeve softly. Do not overfill. Gather around top. Pull up tucking edges inside.

23 Bend arm. Stitch.

24 Position arm onto body side. Pin. Stitch through top into body.

25 CATAPULT
Thread a tiny square of felt onto a piece of strong thread. Tie ends to twig. Curl Wilfred's hand around the twig. Stitch hand. Tidy Wilfred's fur with a brush.

Mrs Apple

Mrs Apple is an extremely kind and homely mouse. She is an
excellent cook and her primrose puddings are
always in demand.

Patterns

All patterns are printed full size. Using tracing paper, carefully trace over each one marking positions of eyes and other details. Cut out tracings.

Leaves

Cut out 6
White card

Apron

Cut out 1

White cotton

Hat crown

Cut out 1

Straw-coloured
open weave

Pocket

Cut out 2

White
cotton

Bib

Cut out 2

White cotton

Materials

1 Two pipe cleaners.
2 Straw-coloured open weave fabric 33 cm × 13 cm (13 in × 5 in).
  Choose a soft medium weight dress fabric or embroidery fabric,
  e.g. flax, linen or canvas. Wash before using to soften.
3 Brown fur fabric 23 cm × 11.4 cm (9 in × 4½ in).
  Dense pile no more than 8 mm ($\frac{5}{16}$ in) deep.
4 Blue-striped cotton 68 cm × 16 cm (27 in × 6½ in).
  If blue and white stripes are not available use a small pattern
  in a similar colour, e.g. blue flowers or spots on white.
5 White satin ribbon 53 cm (21 in) long, 6 mm (¼ in) wide.
6 Beige felt 18 cm × 18 cm (7 in × 7 in).
7 Two black beads 6 mm (¼ in) diameter.
8 White cotton fabric 58 cm × 15 cm (23 in × 6 in).
9 Natural raffia. Sold by the bundle in gardening shops.
10 Guipure lace 46 cm (18 in) long, 10 mm ($\frac{3}{8}$ in) wide.
11 White fabric flowers 20 mm (¾ in) diameter. Can be bought
  by the spray in florists' shops. Colour with felt pens.
  Thin white card, glue, toy filling, dark green, blue and pink felt pens.

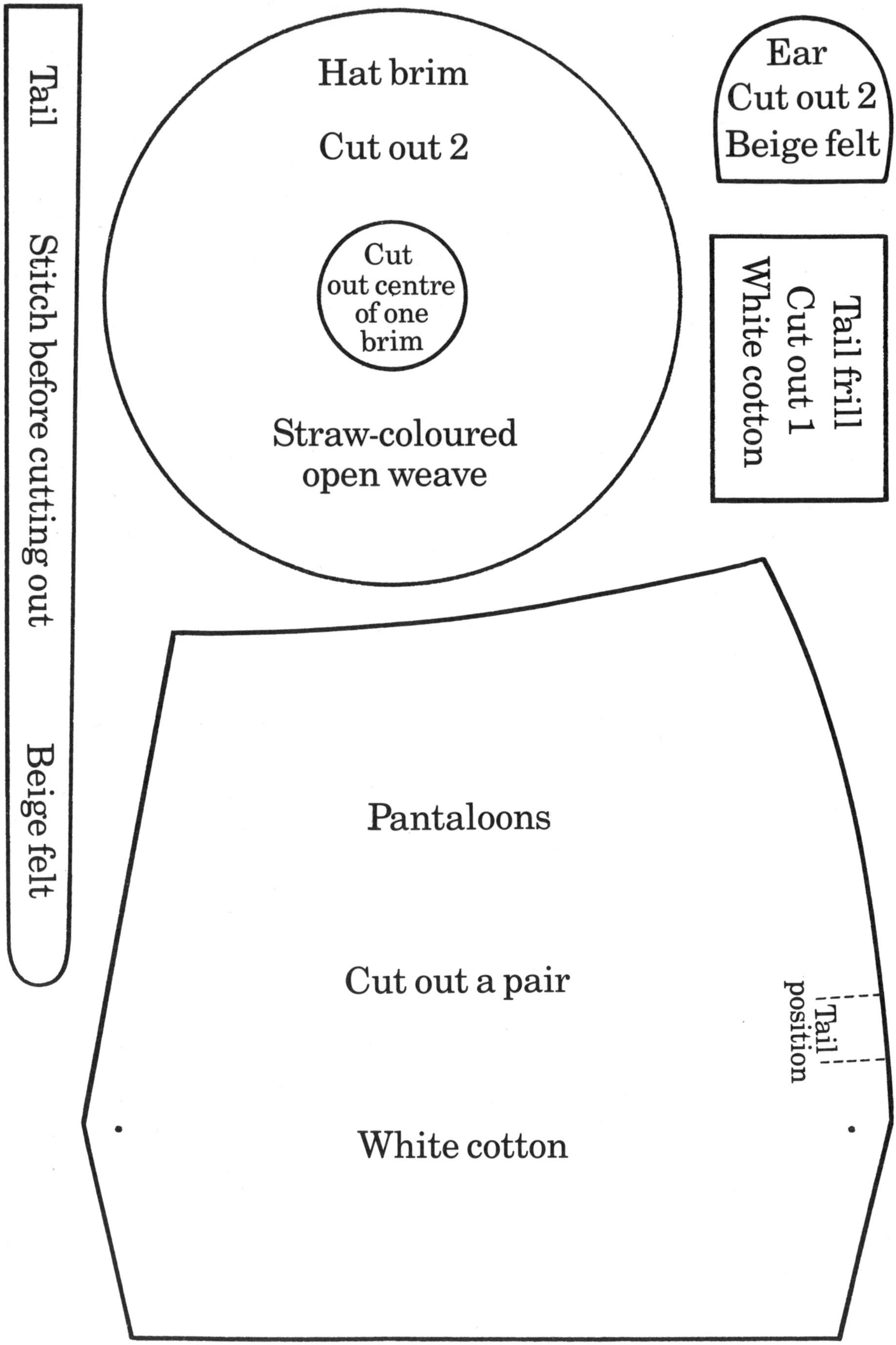

Hat brim

Cut out 2

Cut out centre of one brim

Straw-coloured open weave

Ear
Cut out 2
Beige felt

Tail frill
Cut out 1
White cotton

Tail

Stitch before cutting out

Beige felt

Pantaloons

Cut out a pair

Tail position

White cotton

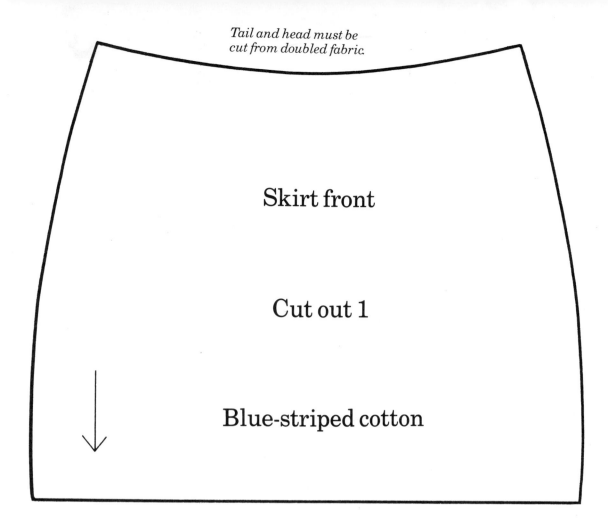

*Tail and head must be
cut from doubled fabric.*

Skirt front

Cut out 1

Blue-striped cotton

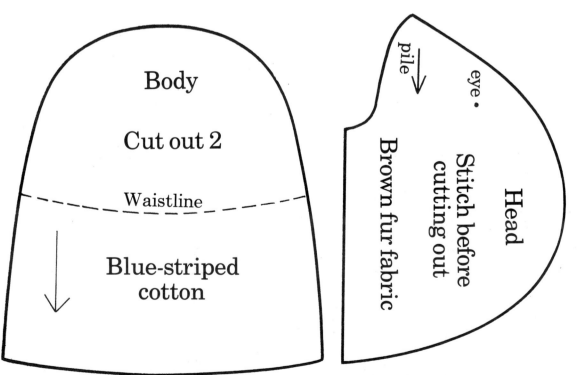

Body

Cut out 2

Waistline

Blue-striped
cotton

pile

eye

Head

Stitch before
cutting out

Brown fur fabric

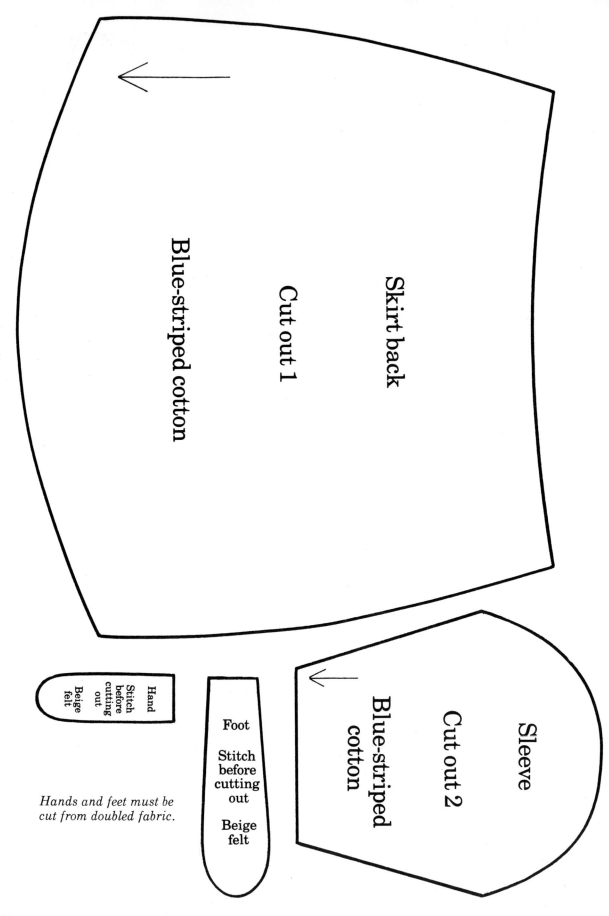

Skirt back

Cut out 1

Blue-striped cotton

Sleeve

Cut out 2

Blue-striped cotton

Hand

Stitch before cutting out

Beige felt

Foot

Stitch before cutting out

Beige felt

Hands and feet must be cut from doubled fabric.

Instructions
for making up

Instructions for head, tail, tail frill, hands, feet and pantaloons on pages 7, 8, 9 and 10. Seams, hems and gathers are 6 mm ($\frac{1}{4}$ in) from the edge. Match pieces with right sides together. Finished height 184 mm ($7\frac{1}{4}$ in).

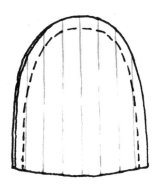

1 BODY
Match pieces. Stitch. Trim away edge. Turn onto right side.

2 Fill firmly up to edge. Gather around. Pull up tight to close.

◁ **3 PANTALOONS**
Fill legs around pipe cleaners and up to 25 mm (1 in) from the top. Use enough filling to hold shape well. Gather around pantaloon top leaving 38 mm ($1\frac{1}{2}$ in) of the front ungathered. Fold top inside on the gather line. Sit body centrally into pantaloons. Match front pantaloon top to waistline on body. Pin. Add more filling under body if necessary. Push more filling into sides and back.

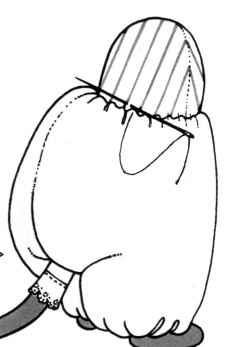

4 Pull up gathers to fit body, matching ▷ pantaloon top to waistline. Stitch top to body.

◁ **5** Take head and sit gathered area onto body. Beginning with large loose stitches in the centre of both, pull head to body comfortably. Stitch around again.

6 APRON BIB
Match pieces. Stitch three sides. Trim ▷ away three edges. Turn onto right side. Iron.

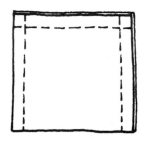

7 STRAPS

Cut two pieces of ribbon 102 mm (4 in) long. Fold one ribbon in half lengthways. Iron. Repeat with other ribbon.

8 Position straps and bib onto body ▷ overlapping pantaloon top. Stitch ends and corners to pantaloons and body.

9 SKIRT

Match pieces. Stitch sides. Fold up bottom edge. Stitch. Gather around top leaving 38 mm (1½ in) of the front ungathered. Turn onto right side.

10 Slip skirt onto Mrs Apple. Fold top inside on gathers. Pin front. Pull up gathers to fit body tightly over pantaloons. Stitch skirt top to body.

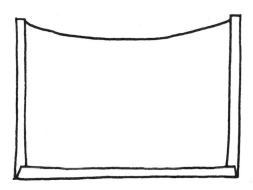

11 APRON
Turn three sides of apron. Iron

13 POCKETS
Fold over top edge. Iron. Gather around curve at very edge. Pull up gathers enough to turn edge onto wrong side.

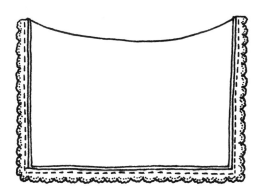

12 Lay guipure lace onto wrong side of apron with edge overhanging apron edge. Stitch.

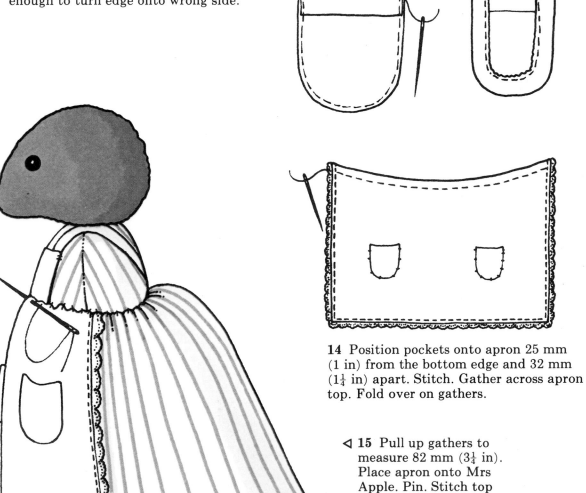

14 Position pockets onto apron 25 mm (1 in) from the bottom edge and 32 mm ($1\frac{1}{4}$ in) apart. Stitch. Gather across apron top. Fold over on gathers.

◁ **15** Pull up gathers to measure 82 mm ($3\frac{1}{4}$ in). Place apron onto Mrs Apple. Pin. Stitch top to body.

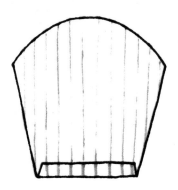

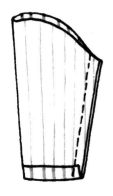

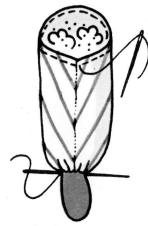

16 SLEEVES
Fold up bottom edge. Iron.

17 Fold to match sides. Stitch. Turn onto right side.

18 Gather around sleeve bottom on fold. Pop hand inside with 20 mm ($\frac{3}{4}$ in) showing. Pull up tight. Take stitches through hand. Fill sleeve softly. Do not overfill. Gather around top. Pull up, tucking edges inside.

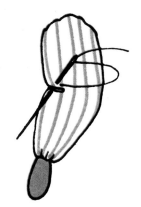

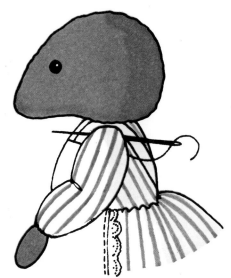

◁ **20** Position arm onto body side. Pin. Stitch through top into body.

19 Bend arm. Stitch.

◁ **21 BOW**
Cut a piece of ribbon 31 cm (12 in) long. Tie bow. Glue bow to waist at centre of back.

22 HAT Brim
Do not forget to cut out ▷ center of one brim piece. Match pieces. Stitch. Trim away edge close to stitches. Turn onto right side. Iron.

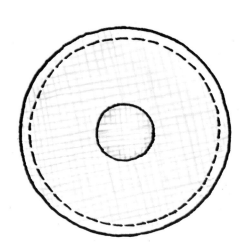

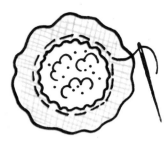

23 HAT Crown
Gather edge. Pull up
slightly. Fill centre enough
to hold shape. Pull up
gathers until edges meet.

24 Position crown over
hole in brim. Pin together
comfortably. Stitch. Sit hat
on top of head. Press down.
Pin. With a long needle,
stitch through crown/brim
join into head.

25 EARS
Fold ear bottom in half.
Stitch on edge.

26 Position ears onto brim at sides of
crown. Stitch ear bottoms to brim.

27 LEAVES
Cut leaves out of thin card. Colour both
sides with a dark green felt pen.

28 FLOWERS
Colour flowers with felt pens. Glue flowers
and leaves around hat over crown/brim join.

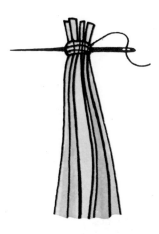

31 Coil plait, tucking end under and butting edges together. Stitch between edges.

29 BASKET

Take six 102 cm (40 in) lengths of raffia. If lengths are not long enough, tie two together and hide the knot in the plaiting. Secure ends.

◁ **30** Pin end to a soft surface. Make a flat 6 mm ($\frac{1}{4}$ in) wide plait. Iron finished plait through a damp cloth.

32 Coil until base measures 32 mm ($1\frac{1}{4}$ in) diameter.

33 Turn plait up at rightangles to base, butting edges. Stitch between edges.

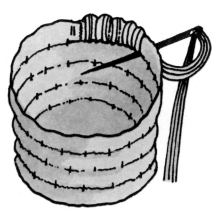

34 Coil until side reaches 25 mm (1 in) high. Trim and stitch plait end to the inside. Thread needle with raffia. Stitch over the top edge to form a neat tight rim.

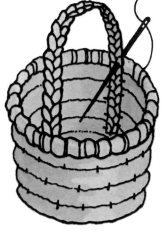

35 HANDLE

Take six strands of raffia, plait very tightly until 11 cm ($4\frac{3}{8}$ in) long. Position ends inside basket. Stitch. Curl Mrs Apple's hand around handle. Stitch. Tidy Mrs Apple's fur with a brush.

Dusty Dogwood

Dusty Dogwood is in charge of the Flour Mill and supplies Brambly Hedge with poppyseed cakes, clover-petal bread and excellent chestnut rolls.

Patterns

All patterns are printed full size. Using tracing paper, carefully trace over each one marking positions of eyes and other details. Cut out tracings.

Hands and tail must be cut from doubled fabric.

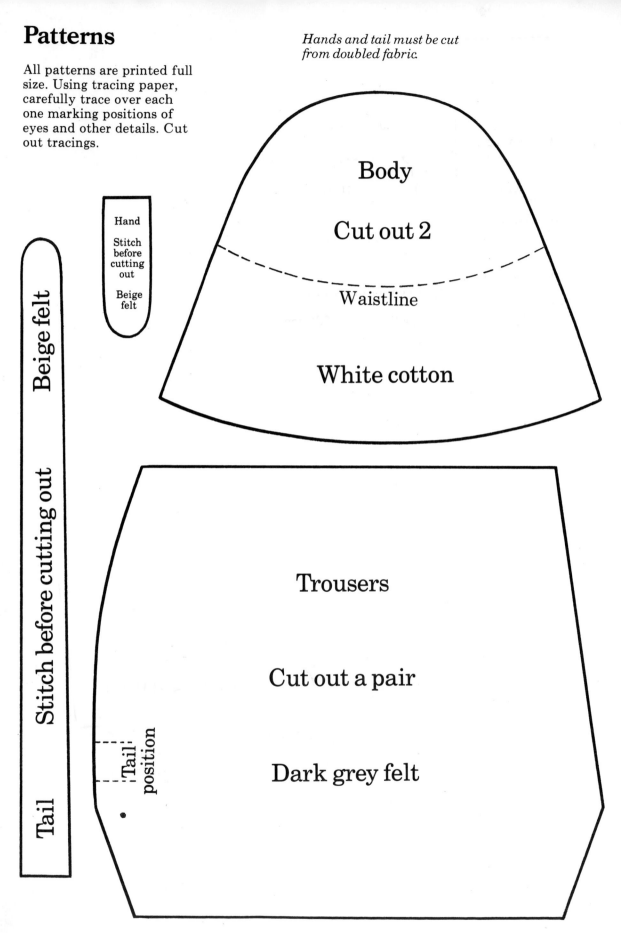

Hand
Stitch before cutting out
Beige felt

Beige felt

Stitch before cutting out

Tail

Body

Cut out 2

Waistline

White cotton

Trousers

Cut out a pair

Dark grey felt

Tail position

Materials

1 Dark grey felt 30 cm × 30 cm (12 in × 12 in).
2 Two pipe cleaners.
3 Brown fur fabric 23 cm × 11.4 cm (9 in × 4½ in). Dense pile no more than 8 mm (⁵⁄₁₆ in) deep.
4 Fabric daisy 38 mm (1½ in) diameter. Can be bought by the spray in florists' shops.
5 White felt 5 cm × 5 cm (2 in × 2 in).
6 Pink felt 9 cm × 9 cm (3½ in × 3½ in).
7 Two black beads 6 mm (¼ in) diameter.
8 Four black beads (very tiny).
9 Beige felt 18 cm × 18 cm (7 in × 7 in).
10 White cotton fabric 30 cm × 11 cm (12 in × 4½ in). Glue, toy filling and a lime green felt pen.

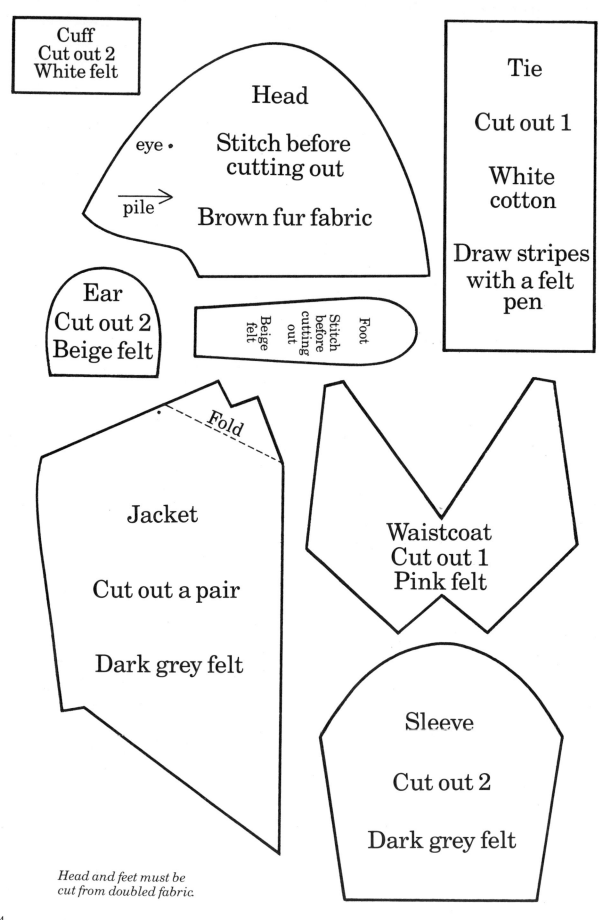

Cuff
Cut out 2
White felt

Head

Stitch before
cutting out

Brown fur fabric

eye •

pile →

Tie

Cut out 1

White
cotton

Draw stripes
with a felt
pen

Ear
Cut out 2
Beige felt

Foot

Stitch
before
cutting
out

Beige
felt

Fold

Jacket

Cut out a pair

Dark grey felt

Waistcoat
Cut out 1
Pink felt

Sleeve

Cut out 2

Dark grey felt

*Head and feet must be
cut from doubled fabric.*

Instructions
for making up

Instructions for head, tail, hands and feet on pages 7, 8 and 9. Seams, hems and gathers are 6 mm ($\frac{1}{4}$ in) from the edge. Match pieces with right sides together. Finished height 184 mm ($7\frac{1}{4}$ in).

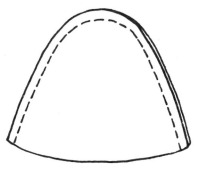

1 BODY
Match pieces. Stitch. Trim away edge. Turn on to right side.

2 Fill firmly up to edge. Gather around. Pull up tight to close.

3 EARS
Fold ear bottom in half. Stitch on edge.

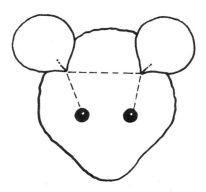

4 Take head and position ears facing forward 25 mm (1 in) above eyes and 38 mm ($1\frac{1}{2}$ in) apart. Pin. Stitch through bottom edges into head. Sit gathered area of head onto body. Beginning with large loose stitches in the centre of both, pull head to body comfortably. Stitch around again.

5 TIE
Draw 3 mm ($\frac{1}{8}$ in) wide lines with a felt pen and ruler onto white cotton tie piece.

6 Fold as illustrated. Iron.

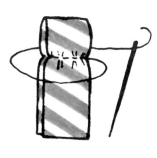

7 Fold in half downwards. Gather across 13 mm ($\frac{1}{2}$ in) from fold. Wrap thread around gathers. Pull up tight. Glue tie to body.

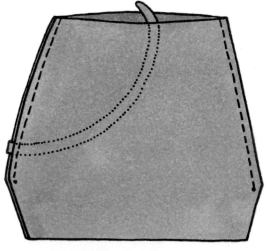

8 TROUSERS
Match pieces with tail between and open end of tail positioned in the back seam. Stitch down to spots.

9 Fold to match inside legs. Stitch. Turn onto right side.

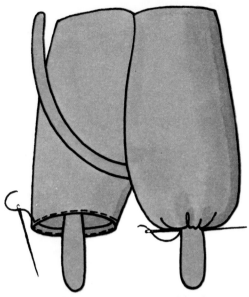

10 Gather around leg. Fold edge inside on gathers. Position foot into leg with 32 mm (1¼ in) showing. Pull up gathers tight. Stitch through the foot at gathers. Bend feet forward.

11 Fill legs around pipe ▷ cleaners and up to 25 mm (1 in) from the top. Use enough filling to hold shape well. Gather around trouser top leaving 38 mm (1½ in) of the front ungathered. Fold top inside on gather line. Sit body centrally into trousers. Match front trouser top to waistline on body. Pin. Add more filling under body if necessary. Push more filling into sides and back.

12 Pull up gathers to fit body, matching trouser top to waistline. Stitch trouser ◁ top to body.

13 WAISTCOAT
Stitch four tiny beads down centre. Position waistcoat onto Dusty's chest. Stitch outer corners to body.

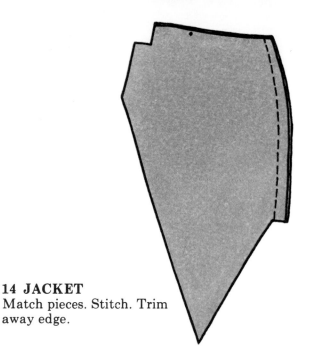

14 JACKET
Match pieces. Stitch. Trim away edge.

15 Fold lapels onto right side. Iron folds through a cloth. Gather across top on very edge between spots. Pull up slightly.

16 Lay jacket centrally onto Dusty's ▷ back, with gathered edge pushed under his head. Pin. Smooth jacket around his waist towards the front. Pin.

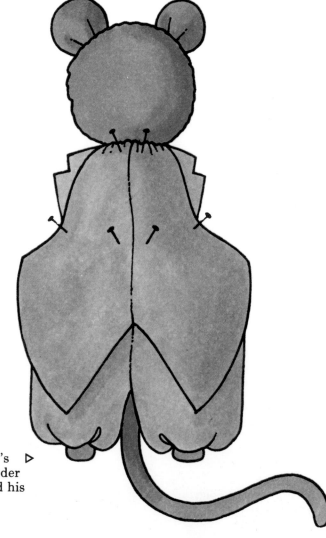

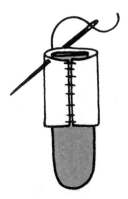

18 CUFFS
Wrap cuff around hand.
Stitch edges and through
hand at the top to hold.

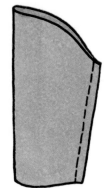

19 SLEEVES
Fold sleeve. Stitch.
Trim away edge. Turn onto
right side.

17 Stitch the jacket to the
body behind the lapels on
both sides.

20 Apply glue to the top edge of the cuff.
Drop hand into sleeve, pulling through
the bottom by catching with the point of
a needle. Do not squeeze the sleeve, the
glue will hold where it touches. Fill sleeve
very softly. Do not overfill. Gather
around top. Pull up tight, tucking
edges inside.

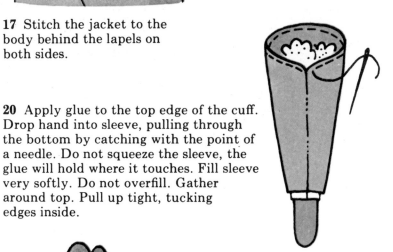

21 Bend arm. Stitch.

22 Position arm onto body side.
Pin. Stitch through top into body.

23 Glue daisy to left lapel. Tidy
Dusty's fur with a brush.

Poppy Eyebright

*Poppy Eyebright was married on Midsummer's Day. She and
Dusty Dogwood exchanged their vows on a floating raft
which was tethered down by the stream and decorated
with honeysuckle and roses.*

Patterns

All patterns are printed full size. Using tracing paper, carefully trace over each one marking positions of eyes and other details. Cut out tracings.

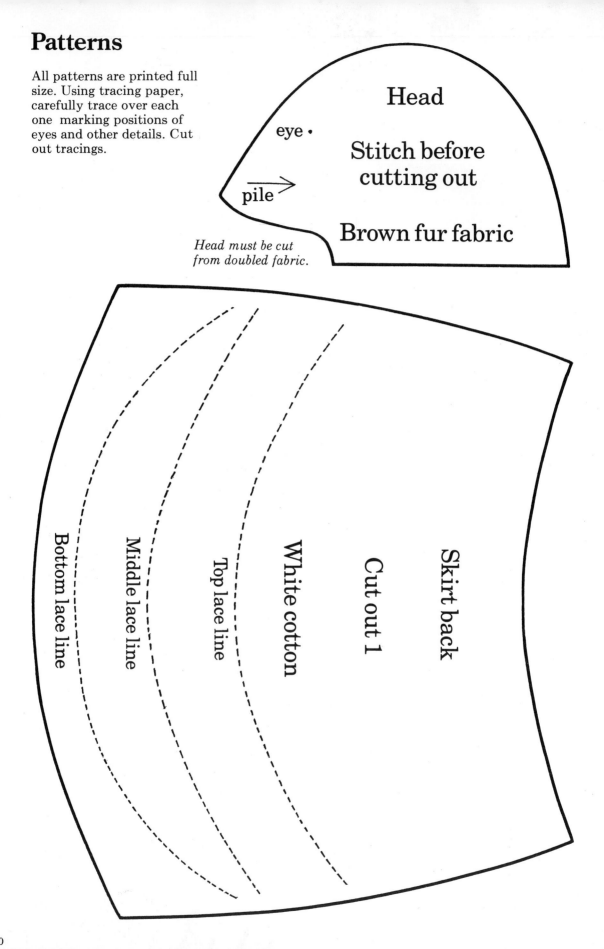

Head

eye •

pile →

Stitch before cutting out

Brown fur fabric

Head must be cut from doubled fabric.

Bottom lace line

Middle lace line

Top lace line

White cotton

Cut out 1

Skirt back

Materials

1   Straw-coloured openweave fabric 33 cm × 13 cm (13 in × 5 in).
Choose a soft medium weight dress fabric or embroidery fabric,
e.g. flax, linen or canvas. Wash before using to soften.

2   White cotton fabric 90 cm × 23 cm (36 in × 9 in).

3   Beige felt 18 cm × 18 cm (7 in × 7 in).

4   White satin ribbon 71 cm (28 in) long, 6 mm ($\frac{1}{4}$ in) wide.

5   Broderie anglaise lace 122 cm (48 in) long, 35 mm ($1\frac{3}{8}$ in) wide after
raw edge has been trimmed. Choose a design with very small cutouts.

6   White fabric flowers 20 mm ($\frac{3}{4}$ in) diameter. Can be bought by the
spray in florists' shops. Colour with felt pens.

7   Pink-striped cotton 61 cm × 13 cm (24 in × 5 in).
If pink and white stripes are not available use a small pattern
in a similar colour, e.g. pink flowers or spots on white.

8   Brown fur fabric 23 cm × 11.4 cm (9 in × $4\frac{1}{2}$ in).
Dense pile no more than 8 mm ($\frac{5}{16}$ in) deep.

9   Guipure lace 76 cm (30 in) long, 10 mm ($\frac{3}{8}$ in) wide.

10   Two pipe cleaners.

11   Embroidery silks. Green, blue and pink.

12   Two black beads 6 mm ($\frac{1}{4}$ in) diameter.
Thin white card, glue, toy filling, dark green, blue and pink felt pens.

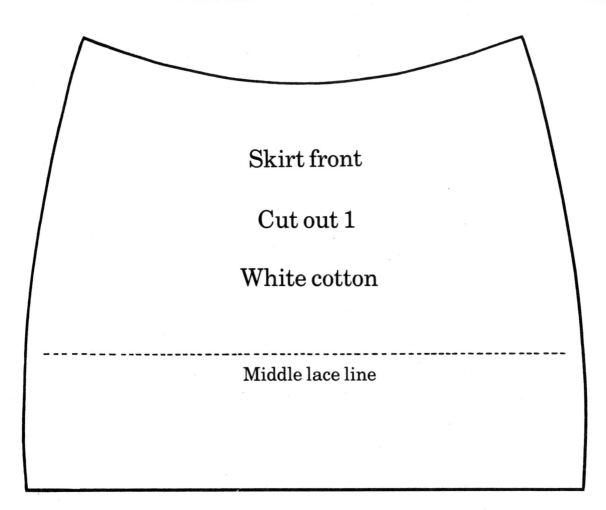

Skirt front

Cut out 1

White cotton

- -

Middle lace line

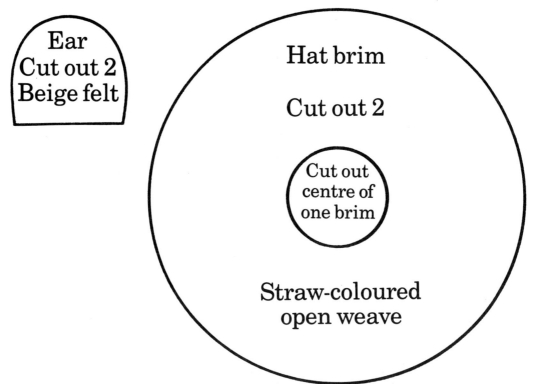

Ear
Cut out 2
Beige felt

Hat brim

Cut out 2

Cut out
centre of
one brim

Straw-coloured
open weave

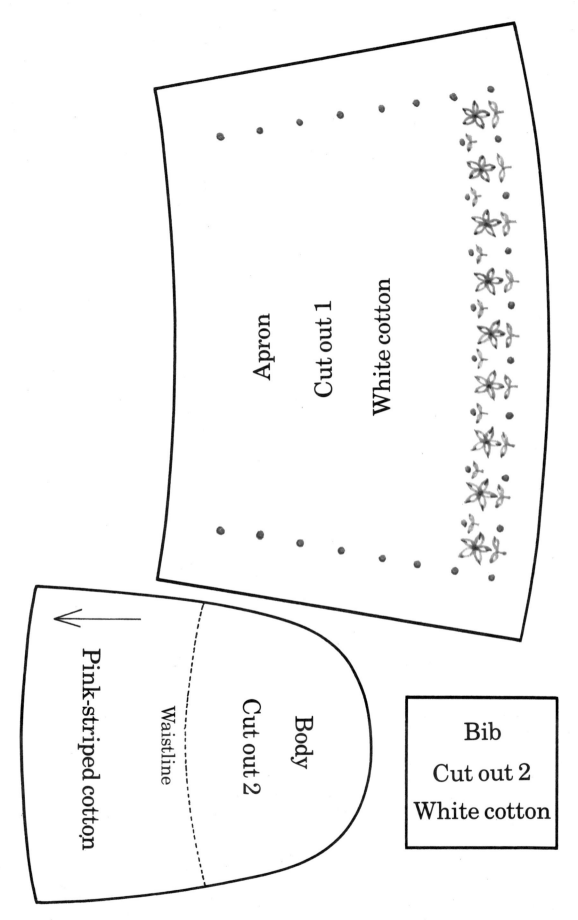

Apron

Cut out 1

White cotton

Pink-striped cotton

Waistline

Body
Cut out 2

Bib

Cut out 2

White cotton

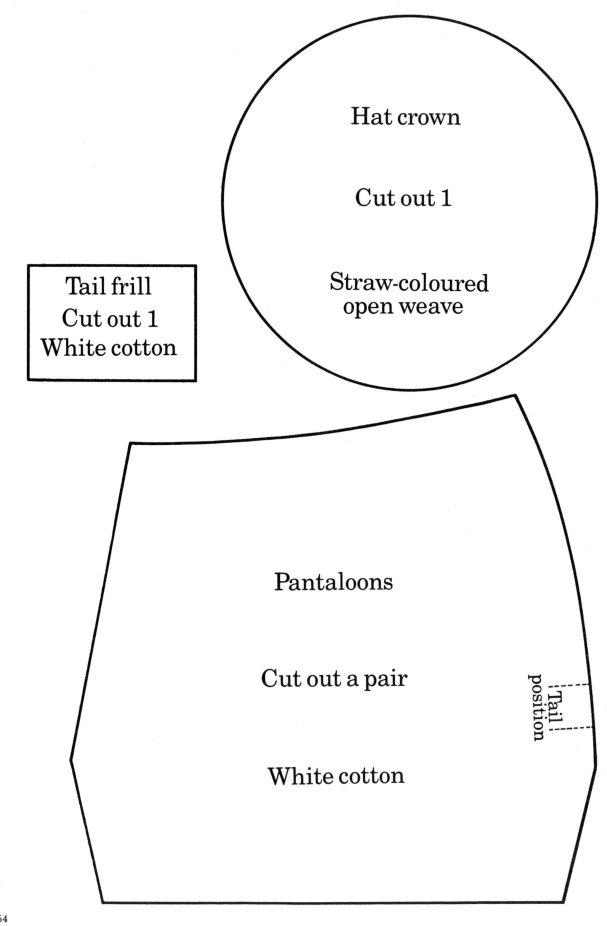

Hat crown

Cut out 1

Straw-coloured
open weave

Tail frill
Cut out 1
White cotton

Pantaloons

Cut out a pair

Tail
position

White cotton

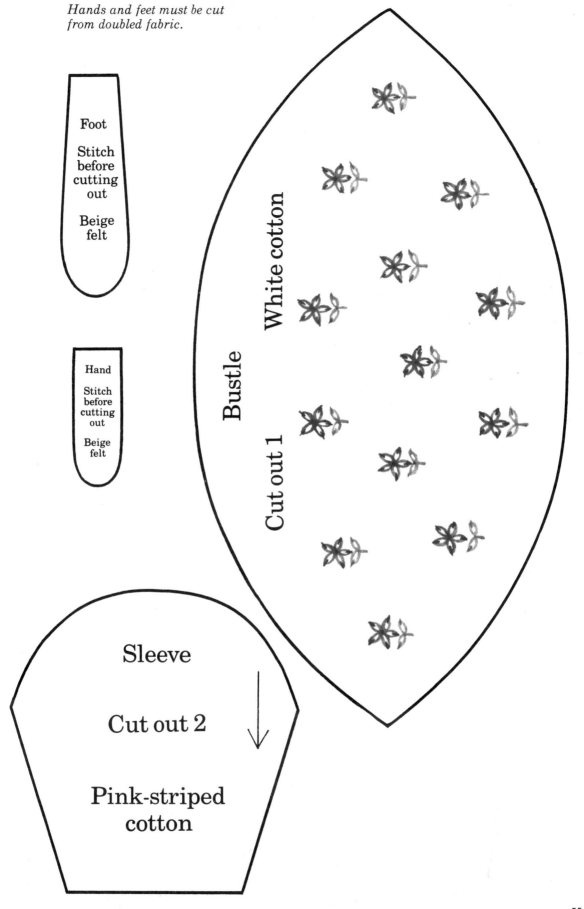

Hands and feet must be cut from doubled fabric.

Foot

Stitch before cutting out

Beige felt

Hand

Stitch before cutting out

Beige felt

Bustle

White cotton

Cut out 1

Sleeve

Cut out 2

Pink-striped cotton

leaves
Cut out 6

White card

Tail must be cut from doubled fabric.

Tail

Stitch before cutting out

Beige felt

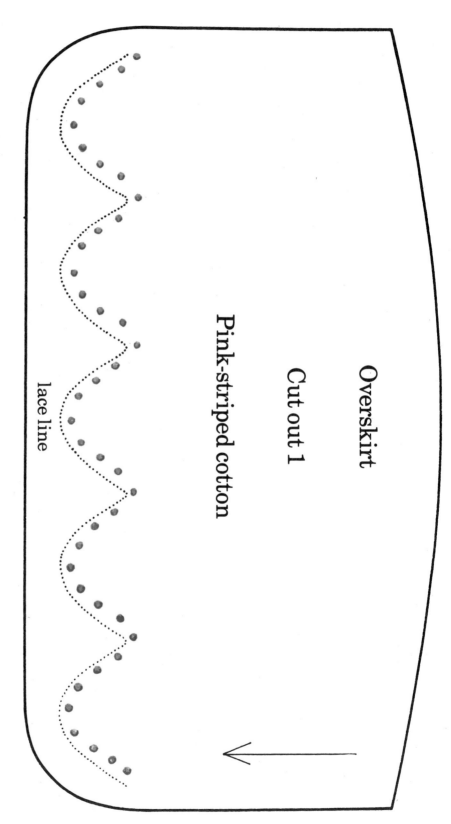

lace line

Pink-striped cotton

Cut out 1

Overskirt

Instructions
for making up

Instructions for head, tail, tail frill, hands, feet and pantaloons on pages 7, 8, 9 and 10. Seams, hems and gathers are 6 mm ($\frac{1}{4}$ in) from the edge. Match pieces with right sides together. Finished height 184 mm ($7\frac{1}{4}$ in).

1 BODY
Match pieces. Stitch. Trim away edge. Turn onto right side.

2 Fill firmly up to edge. Gather around. Pull up tight to close.

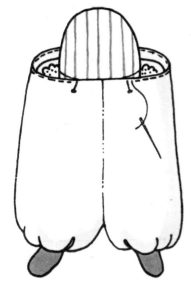

◁ 3 PANTALOONS
Fill legs around pipe cleaners and up to 25 mm (1 in) from the top. Use enough filling to hold shape well. Gather around pantaloon top leaving 38 mm ($1\frac{1}{2}$ in) of the front ungathered. Fold top inside on the gather line. Sit body centrally into pantaloons. Match front pantaloon top to waistline on body. Pin. Add more filling under body if necessary. Push more filling into sides and back.

4 Pull up gathers to fit body, matching ▷ pantaloon top to waistline. Stitch top to body.

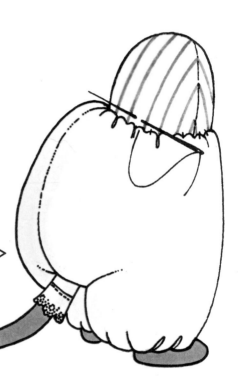

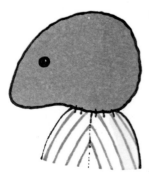

◁ 5 Take head and sit gathered area onto body. Beginning with large loose stitches in the centre of both, pull head to body comfortably. Stitch around again.

6 APRON BIB
Match pieces. Stitch three sides. Trim △ away three edges. Turn onto right side. Iron.

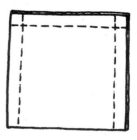

7 STRAPS

Cut two pieces of ribbon 102 mm (4 in) long. Fold one ribbon in half lengthways. Iron. Repeat with other ribbon.

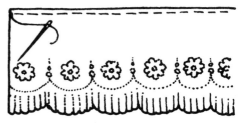

△ 8 Position straps and bib onto body overlapping pantaloon top. Stitch ends and corners to pantaloons and body.

10 Cut a piece of broderie anglaise lace △ 41 cm (16 in) long. Trim away the raw edge to measure 35 mm ($1\frac{3}{8}$ in) at the widest point. Gather along lace 3 mm ($\frac{1}{8}$ in) from the edge. Pull up to measure 20.3 cm (8 in).

△ 9 SKIRT

Mark lace lines onto right sides of skirt pieces. Match pieces. Stitch sides. Fold up bottom edge. Stitch. Turn onto right side.

11 Match gathered edge ▷ of lace to bottom lace line across skirt back with short ends of lace matching middle lace line across skirt front. Spread gathers evenly. Pin. Hand stitch lace to skirt through gathers and short ends.

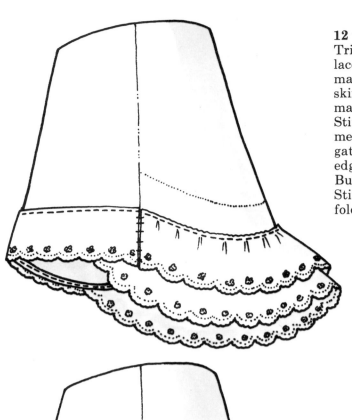

12 Cut a piece of lace 46cm (18 in) long. Trim as before. Fold both short ends of lace onto wrong side. Without gathering, match top of flat lace to lace line across skirt front, beginning with the folded end matched to the side seam of the skirt. Stitch lace to skirt front. Where lace meets the other side seam of skirt, begin gathering remaining lace. Match gathered edge to middle lace line across skirt back. Butt folded ends. Pull up gathers to fit. Stitch through gathers and between folded ends.

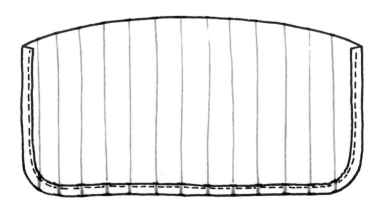

△ **14** Gather around skirt top, leaving 38 mm (1½ in) of the front ungathered. Slip skirt onto Poppy. Fold top inside on gathers. Pin front. Pull up gathers to fit body tightly over pantaloons. Stitch skirt top to body.

△ **13** Cut a piece of lace 31 cm (12 in) long. Trim as before. Gather. Pull up to measure 16.5 cm (6½ in). Match to top lace line across skirt back. Stitch through gathers and short ends.

15 OVERSKIRT
Turn three sides. Stitch. ▷

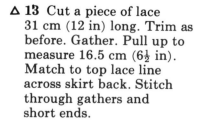

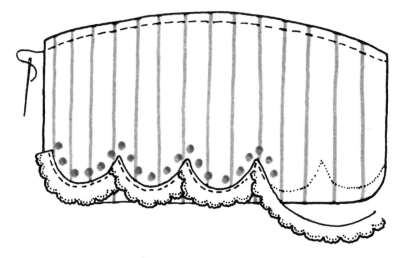

16 Match guipure lace to the line on the right side of overskirt, folding into points. Stitch. Embroider french knots 3 mm ($\frac{1}{8}$ in) from the lace and 6 mm ($\frac{1}{4}$ in) apart. (See detail 17.) Gather across overskirt top.

17 FRENCH KNOT
Use six strands of embroidery silk. Bring needle through fabric where knot is required. Encircle the needle twice with silk. Pull silk tightly around the needle. Take needle back into the fabric close to where it came from. Keep your thumb on the knot whilst pulling the silk through.

18 Fold top of overskirt onto wrong side on gather line. Pull up to measure 82 mm ($3\frac{1}{4}$ in). Position onto Poppy's back, pressing well down on top of skirt. Spread gathers evenly. Pin. Stitch top to body.

19 BUSTLE

Mark embroidery pattern onto bustle.
Fold up bottom edge. Stitch.

20 DAISY STITCH

Use three strands of silk for flowers,
leaves and stems. Bring needle through
the centre of the marked flower. Forming
a loop, take the needle in again at the
centre and out at the required length of
the petal. Take the needle back into the
fabric outside the loop and return to the
centre. Stitch the leaves in the same way.
The stem is a single straight stitch.

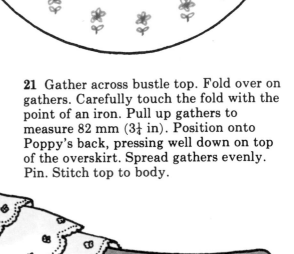

21 Gather across bustle top. Fold over on
gathers. Carefully touch the fold with the
point of an iron. Pull up gathers to
measure 82 mm ($3\frac{1}{4}$ in). Position onto
Poppy's back, pressing well down on top
of the overskirt. Spread gathers evenly.
Pin. Stitch top to body.

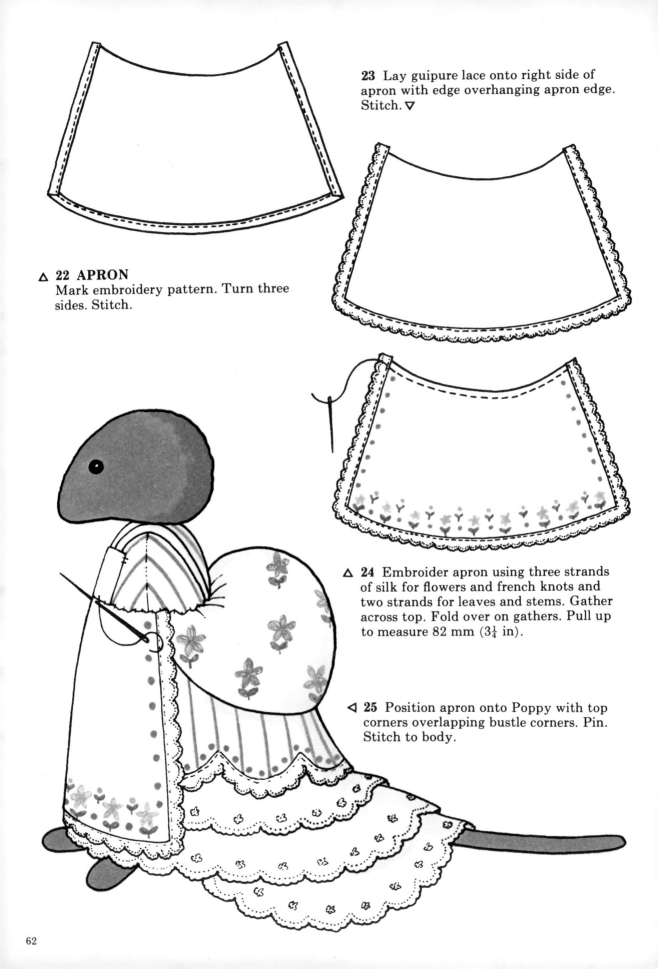

23 Lay guipure lace onto right side of apron with edge overhanging apron edge. Stitch. ▽

△ **22 APRON**
Mark embroidery pattern. Turn three sides. Stitch.

△ **24** Embroider apron using three strands of silk for flowers and french knots and two strands for leaves and stems. Gather across top. Fold over on gathers. Pull up to measure 82 mm (3¼ in).

◁ **25** Position apron onto Poppy with top corners overlapping bustle corners. Pin. Stitch to body.

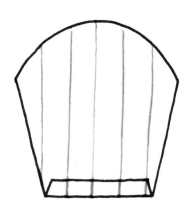

26 SLEEVES
Fold up bottom edge.
Iron.

27 Fold to match sides.
Stitch. Turn onto right
side.

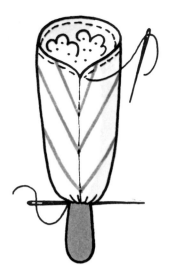

28 Gather around sleeve
bottom on the fold. Pop
hand inside with 20 mm
($\frac{3}{4}$ in) showing. Pull up
tight. Take stitches
through hand. Fill sleeve
softly. Do not overfill.
Gather around top. Pull
up, tucking edges inside.

29 Bend arm.
Stitch.

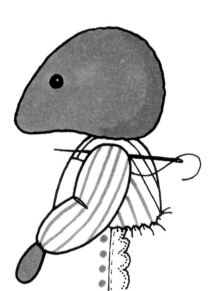

30 Position arm onto body
side. Pin. Stitch through
top into body.

◁ **31 BOW**
Cut a piece of ribbon 31 cm
(12 in) long. Tie bow. Glue
bow to waist at centre of
back over bustle.

32 HAT Brim
Do not forget to cut out ▷
the centre of one brim
piece. Match pieces. Stitch.
Trim away edge close to
stitches. Turn onto right
side. Iron.

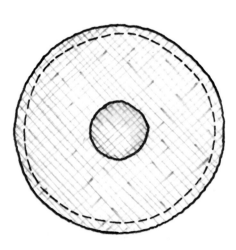

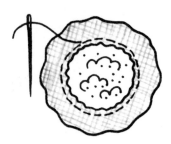

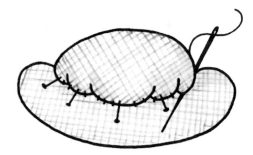

33 HAT Crown
Gather edge. Pull up
slightly. Fill centre enough
to hold shape. Pull up
gathers until edges meet.

34 Position crown over hole in brim. Pin
together comfortably. Stitch. Sit hat on
top of head. Press down. Pin. With a long
needle, stitch through crown/brim join
into head.

35 EARS
Fold ear bottom in half.
Stitch on edge.

36 Position ears onto brim at sides of
crown. Stitch ear bottoms to brim.

37 LEAVES
Cut leaves out of thin card.
Colour both sides with a
dark green felt pen.

38 FLOWERS AND RIBBON
Cut a ribbon 18 cm (7 in) long. Fold in ▷
half. Glue fold to brim back in centre.
Colour flowers with felt pens. Glue flowers
and leaves around hat over crown/brim
join. Tidy Poppy's fur with a brush.